History of Kennin-ji

Period	Western Calendar	Important Events
Kamakura 1185–1333	1202	Upon returning from China, Yosai founded Kennin-ji under the patronage of Minamoto no Yoriie (1182–1204), the second Kamakura shogun. Initially, Zen, Tendai, and Shingon Buddhism were all practiced concurrently.
	1205	Construction was completed, and Kennin-ji became a state-sponsored temple.
	1215	Yosai died at Kennin-ji (although according to one theory, he passed away at Jufuku-ji in Kamakura).
	1246	Temple buildings were destroyed by fire. Rankei Doyru arrived in Japan.
	1258	Many of the buildings were rebuilt by the tenth abbot Enni Benen.
Muromachi 1336–1573	1342	Kennin-ji was ranked fourth of Kyoto's Five Great Zen Temples by the shogunate.
	1386	Kennin-ji was ranked third among Kyoto's Five Great Zen Temples.
	1469	Massive destruction caused by fires resulting from the Onin Bunmei War.
	1552	The main temple buildings were completely destroyed in battle and many of the sub-temples were lost.
Azuchi momoyama 1573–1603	1586	Shogun Toyotomi Hideyoshi contributed enough rice to feed 820 people for one year to the temple.
Edo 1603–1868	1614	Shogun Tokugawa Ieyasu donated enough rice to feed 820 people for one year to the temple.
Meiji 1868–1912	1872	Kyoto's Five Great Zen Temples, along with Daitoku-ji and Myoshin-ji, comprised to form the so-called seven factions. Kennin-ji took the name of the Kennin-ji School. The first chief abbot was Keiso Tobun.
Showa 1926–89	1934	The Abbot's Quarters (Hojo) were destroyed by Typhoon Muroto, and the temple compound suffered extensive damage.
	1964	A semicentennial memorial service commemorated the 750th anniversary of the death of Yosai, the temple's founder.
Heisei 1989–2019	2002	*Twin Dragons* was painted on the ceiling of the Dharma Hall (Hatto) in commemoration of the 800th anniversary of the temple's founding.

Terminology

1. Sub-temple (*Tacchu*)
A *tacchu* is a sub-temple located within the precincts of a major Buddhist temple. Originally, the tacchu developed around the tombs of important abbots, but most present *tacchu* began as residences of eminent priests or as memorial temples for aristocratic families.

2. Aureola (*Kohai*)
A decoration on the back of a Buddhist statue symbolizing the light that emits from the body of the Buddha.

3. Tea Ceremony (*Sarei*)
Sarei is a ritual practice fundamental to the daily ascetic discipline of the Zen monk and is carried out several times each day.

4. The Flower Sermon (*Nengemisho*)
A legend that teaches the origins of Zen Buddhism. It is said that when the Buddha silently showed a lotus flower to his disciples, they could not comprehend its meaning and stayed silent; only Mahakasyapa smiled in understanding. The Truth of Buddhism cannot be expressed in words, but is instructed through the silence of Mahakasyapa. Hence, this story is used in Zen to convey an understanding of the dharma through non-verbal transmission.

5. Zen Master (*Zenji*)
An honorary title related to a high-ranking priest of Zen Buddhism, especially that which designates a person who has had a title bestowed upon them from the Imperial Court.

Notations in this book
Buildings, artwork, and artifacts that are designated as National Treasures are indicated with a red diamond (◆) and Important Cultural Properties, in blue (◆). Terminology is annotated on page 1 (English) and 32 (Japanese). Specialized Buddhist terminology is provided in Romanized Japanese. Names of individuals are expressed in the traditional Japanese order, with last name followed by first. Ages of individuals are expressed by the Japanese system, in which one's first year is counted as year one.

The Rinzai School of Zen Buddhism: Beginnings

Master Yosai—The Priest Who Brought Zen from China

Following the stone-paved streets of Hanami-koji in Kyoto's Gion district, the unassuming gate of Kennin-ji appears and one is suddenly drawn onto the temple grounds.

As Kyoto's most ancient zen temple, the history of Kennin-ji reaches back over 800 years and is formally known as the "headquarters of the Rinzai school, Kennin-ji branch of Zen Buddhism, Tozan, Kennin-ji." The temple sits nearby Yasaka Shrine and Maruyama Park, both famous sightseeing spots where, all year round, the streams of tourists never subside. Kennin-ji's location—adjoining the old geisha district of Gion—and its status as a Zen temple of harsh ascetic discipline, is thought to be an amusing combination.

In spite of its being downtown, Kennin-ji's inner grounds are comfortably spacious and the greenery of the pines and tea plants is utterly refreshing. Lined to the north and south of the center are monastic buildings characteristic of Zen temples. The reverent atmosphere of the Founder's Hall (Kaisando) and sub-temples (*tacchu*¹) envelop the scene. Even to this day, one can feel the resonant traditions of the Zen sanctuary.

Kennin-ji's founder Yosai (also read Eisai; 1141–1215; 4) was born the son of a Shinto priest at Kibitsu Shrine in present day Okayama prefecture. He learned the foundations of Buddhism from his father and was already reading philosophical texts at eight years old. He then studied Tendai Buddhism and received his full precepts at Enryaku-ji, the Tendai headquarters on Mount Hiei in northern Kyoto, at the age of fourteen.

The late Heian period (794–1185), when Yosai was on Mount Hiei, was marked by a sense of spiritual foreboding that stemmed from the belief that the world had entered the age of destruction that was taught in the Buddhist doctrine. Serious monks like Yosai were also concerned that life on Mount Hiei—originally intended to exemplify true Buddhist practice—had become lax and worldly as many important positions at the temple were being filled with family members of the aristocracy.

1. Imperial Messenger Gate (Chokushimon)

1

Imperial Messenger Gate (Chokushimon)

13c. ◆

Copper-tiled, four-pillared gate with a gabled roof.

2

Dharma Hall (Hatto); Twin Dragons decorative ceiling painting

Painting by Koizumi Junsaku in commemoration of the 800th anniversary of the founding of Kennin-ji. The twin dragons represent the beginning and end of all things (*A-un*) and together, work to protect Buddhism.

2. Dharma Hall (Hatto); Twin Dragons decorative ceiling painting

About **Kennin-ji**

In 1168, at the age of twenty-eight, Yosai traveled to China to study Chinese Buddhism for six months. There, he discovered Rinzai Zen and was impressed by its vigor. At forty-seven, Yosai again traveled to China to practice in the Yellow Dragon (Huanglong) lineage of Rinzai Zen. After for four years of study with Abbot Kian Ejo, he was awarded priest's robes as proof of his permission to teach Rinzai Zen of the Yellow Dragon lineage.

Connection with the Kamakura Shogunate

When Yosai returned to Japan, he traveled to the Hirado domain (modern-day Nagasaki prefecture) and established the first place in Japan dedicated to living daily life according to Zen principles.

Yosai next traveled to Kyoto to begin proselytizing, but was thwarted by stalwarts of traditional Buddhism, such as that on Mount Hiei, and the Imperial Court ordered a halt to Zen Buddhism. He reluctantly returned to Kyushu and, four years later, arrived in Kamakura where the samurai were centered. Eventually, Yosai received tremendous conversions from the samurai, whose sensibilities were well suited to the new Zen teachings.

Yosai had the deep trust of Minamoto no Yoriie (1182–1204; 3), the second Kamakura shogun. In 1200, Yosai was entreated to be the founding abbot of Kamakura's Jufuku-ji by Hojo Masako (1157–1225), wife of the first shogun, and, two years later, Yoriie founded Kennin-ji in Kyoto. The Imperial Court bestowed the name of Kennin era on the temple, just as it had for Enryaku-ji during the Enryaku era. Both temples were sponsored by the Kamakura shogunate. Due to initial concerns regarding repercussions from Mount Hiei, teachings were initially focused on the three major Buddhist schools—Zen, Shingon, and Tendai.

Although Yosai himself lived a frugal life, he was often asked for help by the needy. It is said that, to the astonishment of his disciples, he once removed the aureola (*kohai*[2]) from a statue in the Main Hall (Hondo) and gave it away to help the poor.

3. Seated statue of founder Minamoto no Yoriie

3

Seated statue of founder Minamoto no Yoriie

Wood; 73.6cm; 18c.

Seated statue of Minamoto no Yoriie, whose remains are enshrined at Kennin-ji's Founder's Hall (Kaisando) in ceremonial court dress on the occasion of becoming the second Kamakura shogun at twenty-one years old. This statue was made in 1752 in commemoration of the 550th anniversary of his death, and was consecrated the following year.

4

Portrait of Minnan Yosai

Silk; 93 × 38.5cm; 15c. (Ryosoku-in collection)

Oldest extant monk's portrait of Yosai as the founder of Kennin-ji. The abbot of Shokoku-ji in Kyoto, referenced a work from prominent Zen monk Mugaku Sogen (1226–86) when writing the inscription.

鹿苑比丘中津九皋書

二菴仰首塵之讀

佛光國師所讚之牓

謹書

庭仁開山千光祥師頂和

兩國水中之月

千載花上之春道播

法而雷瀉電掣乘雷

壯詞端來三零嗣山

一錫凌滄溟南詢溪

法中之英僧中之傑

4. Portrait of Minnan Yosai

About **Kennin-ji**

From Three Buddhist Schools to a Pure House of Zen Meditation

Yosai passed away in 1215 at the age of seventy-four. At the time, he had 2,000 disciples and disciples of his disciples counted 10,000. In 1259, Rankei Doryu (1213–78) became the eleventh abbot and, finding Kennin-ji to be a place of mixed-Zen practice, instituted reforms to return it to a center for pure Zen meditation. Kennin-ji began to flourish and experienced a golden age marked by its ranking as third of Kyoto's Five Great Zen Temples by the third Ashikaga shogun Yoshimitsu (1358–1408). Five Mountains Literature (Gozan Bungaku) flourished and many high-ranking priests were produced.

With the decline of the shogunate and loss of

6. Toyobo Tea House

5
Daio-en (front garden of the Abbot's Quarters)

White stones are spread across the front expanse, and the contrast of the trees and large stones which rise behind them is strikingly beautiful. The name Daio-en draws from a pseudonym for the majestic mountain Baizhang Shan in Jiangxi, China.

6
Toyobo Tea House

A tea house to the north of the Abbot's Quarters (Hojo). Nearby is the elegant "Kennin-ji fence" made of split-bamboo, which is vertically lined with no spaces in between and held in place with horizontal half-split bamboo.

5. Daio-en (front garden of the Abbot's Quarters)

economic power in the mid-Muromachi period, however, maintenance of deteriorating temple buildings became extremely difficult. Although they encountered numerous difficulties, religious sects banded together to collectively protect Yosai's "light of Buddhism."

Yosai is also famous for bringing the tea ceremony (sarei[3]) that had been practiced in Chinese Zen temples to Japan. He is revered as the patriarch of tea for having planted and cultivated tea seeds brought home from his travels, as well as having instructed people in the ways of drinking tea.

Yosai was lamenting the pitiful state of Buddhism in the latter days of the Heian Period and wanted to breathe a bit of fresh air into the Japanese Buddhist world by bringing Chinese Zen to Japan.

In Zen there is a strong desire to return to the original Buddha, as he is the epitome of the perfection of knowledge. Zen holds seated meditation (*zazen*) in high esteem and takes it as central to its practice because the Buddha, in his youth, achieved enlightenment after stopping his austerities and entering into meditation, and *zazen* is seen as a path by which to achieve enlightenment. Therefore, in most Rinzai Zen temples, a figure of the Buddha as a layman engaged in meditation is enshrined as the main object of worship.

The principal figure in the Dharma Hall (Hatto; 7) is a statue of the Buddha (Shaka Nyorai; 8) sitting in a cross-legged position. His mudra of contemplation (*zenjoin*), and he is flanked by two of his ten primary disciples, Maha Kasyapa and Ananda, as in the case in most Zen temples. Maha Kasyapa is said to have been foremost in removing himself from earthly desires, and Ananda was foremost in hearing and remembering the Buddha's sermons.

Dharma Hall (Hatto)

According to the plaque affixed to the ridgepole at the time of construction, the Dharma Hall was built in 1765. It spans five bays across by four bays deep (about 9 × 7.2m), and features arched windows and a paneled Chinese door at its entrance, both structural components typical of traditional Zen-style architecture. There is a great dignity of spirit that is reflected in the halls other name, Nenge-do, which references *The Flower Sermon* (*Nengemisho*[4]) legend of Buddha's mind-to-mind transmission of wisdom to his disciple Maha Kasyapa.

In 1552 the Buddha Hall (Butsuden) at Kennin-ji was destroyed by the fires of war and was never rebuilt. The Dharma Hall still serves double-duty as the Buddha Hall to this day. At the front of the temple is a seated statue of the Buddha, the principal image, flanked by standing statues of his disciples Maha Kasyapa and Ananda. Enshrined at the adjacent Ancestral Hall (Soshido) is a statue of the founder Yosai.

7. Dharma Hall (Hatto) ; 17-19c.

8

Seated statue of the Buddha (Shaka Nyorai)

Wood; figure height 90.8cm; 14-16c.

The figure sits in a cross-legged position with hands overlapping and joined in front of the abdomen to form the meditation mudra. The meditating figure has an aura of stability, and the deep gaze quiets the mind. This statue was relocated to Kennin-ji from Kosho-ji temple in Fukui prefecture in the latter half of the sixteenth century.

Founder's Hall (Kaisando)

Built as the burial place for Kennin-ji's founder Zen Master Yosai Zenji[5] in 1884. Looking at a ground plan of the hall, the Worship Hall (Raido), Waiting Room (Ai no Ma), and Mortuary Hall (Shido) form a convex pattern with the Worship Hall to the front. This structure is seven bays wide and three deep, and has a hip-and-gable roof with traditional tiles (*hongawarabuki*). Beyond this is the Waiting Room, which houses Yosai's "nirvana entering pagoda." In the innermost point of the structure is the Mortuary Hall, where a wooden statue of Yosai is located.

A Two-story Gate (Romon) called Hodakaku rises at the front of the Founder's Hall (9). This was dismantled and moved from Kyoto's Myoko-ji to coincide with the construction of the Kaisando in 1885. Small structures were built on either side of the gate in the mid-Edo period in order to access the upper floor. Three of the Bodhi trees that Yosai brought back from China still remain in the front garden.

A solemn air always pervades the atmosphere in this most sacred place within the temple grounds, and the chief priests take turns keeping continual watch over it. Because it is generally closed to the public, the Hodakaku gate may only be seen from beyond a fence.

9. Founder's Hall (Kaisando) 19-20c.

10. Interior of the Founder's Hall (Kaisando)

10
Interior of the Founder's Hall (Kaisando)

Square floor tiles are laid on the diagonal, with an octopus-leg incense burner at the center. On a stone altar in the Waiting Room (Ai no Ma) is Yosai's "nirvana entering pagoda." It is enclosed by a wooden fence, with a lamp that burns continuously day and night. A statue of Yosai is located at the top of the stairs in the rear, and a seated statue of Kennin-ji's founder Minamoto no Yoriie wearing ceremonial dress is located on the side platform at the base of the stairs (3).

11
Statue of Yosai Zenji
Wood; 130.8cm; 17-19c.

Carved by Kojo of the renowned Kei school of Buddhist sculptors in 1664, as evidenced by an inscription in the vermillion lacquer carved into the underside of the garment's hem. Yosai wears a ringed monk's stole and is seated in a chair holding a short staff as is typical of monk's portraits.

11. Statue of Yosai Zenji

THE BEAUTY *of* GREAT TREASURE

Tanabe Masako
Chiba City Museum of Arts,
Deputy Director

From its introduction in the early Kamakura period, Zen became the intellectual foundation for samurai and the upper classes. At the same time, the aesthetic consciousness of Zen had a profound impact on such areas as calligraphy, ink painting, and architecture. During the early period of Japanese Zen, important monks such as Kennin-ji's eleventh abbot Rankei Doryu and Issan Ichinei (1247–1317) came to Japan from China. Rankei arrived in Japan at the age of thirty-four, having been invited by a regent to the Kamakura shogun Hojo Tokiyori (1227–63) to both provide personal religious instruction and open Kencho-ji in Kamakura.Rankei's simple monk's stole still stands as a testament to the spirit of Zen simplicity that he both lived by and strictly instilled in his disciples.

The Influence of Zen on Japanese Art

Issan Ichinei also had a profound destiny with Kamakura temples and was the personal religious teacher of Hojo Sadatoki (1271–1311), who established him at Kencho-ji. The calligraphy piece *On a Snowy Night* (*Setsuya no Saku*), composed in 1315, was given to Kennin-ji. It is said to have been composed at the time when Issan was serving as the third abbot of Nanzen-ji in Kyoto. It includes an anecdote about Eka (487–593), the second patriarch of Zen, being buried up to the waist in snow while begging Daruma (?–?), the patriarch of Zen, for entry into his monastery.

The paintings *The Sixteen Arhats* (*rakan*, or disciples of the Buddha; 12, 13) is a masterpiece representative of such paintings in Japan, and depicts standard figures that seem to have been modeled on Chinese works. They are attributed to the painter-priest Ryozen (?–?) of Tofuku-ji in Kyoto, and there are records stating that a monk of Tofuku-ji received solicitations for the their production. Due to these reasons, as well as the message "at Tofuku-ji, in perpetuity" written in gold on the paintings, it is evident that the these were done at Tofuku-ji, and were at one time held there.

Zen

12, 13
The Sixteen Arhats
(12: Chudahantaka, 13: Ingada)
Ryozen; silk; 143.2 × 59.6cm (each scroll); 14c. ◆

Ryozen was a painter specializing in Buddhist paintings at Tofuku-ji, preceding the famous artist-monk Kitsusan Mincho at Tofuku-ji. Each of the sixteen arhats are depicted individually on a width of silk in a typical design; the strength and dignity of the portrayals is a masterpiece. On the right is Ingada, the thirteenth arhat, and on the left is the sixteenth, Chudahantaka.

12. The Sixteen Arhats (Chudahantaka)

13. The Sixteen Arhats (Ingada)

14. The Four Accomplishments (detail)

Four Brilliant Artists

Kaiho Yusho
Tawaraya Sotatsu
Ito Jakuchu
Soga Shohaku

Kaiho Yusho (1533–1615) was born in modern-day Shiga prefecture to a vassal of the high-ranking Azai clan, and his artistic aspirations are thought to be a direct result of war. When his clan fell in 1573, Yusho was the sole survivor of his family. He chose to be neither samurai nor monk, but rather to paint for a living. He then became a pupil of the Kano school, the preeminent painting circle in Japan at the time, and was soon following the styles of famous Chinese painters. He simultaneously established his own style, and became one of the preeminent painters of the day.

Yusho was already sixty-seven years old (quite an advanced age for an artist in those days) when the Abbot's Quarters (Hojo) at Kennin-ji was rebuilt in 1599. He was what one might call a late bloomer, however, for after leaving the Kano school, he had an important period of development during which he painted altogether fifty images on sliding screens in the Abbot's Quarters.

Many of Yusho's works, such as *The Four Accomplishments* (14), are similar to the Kano school style. However, it is in works like the simply drawn, thick outlines of the oversized "bag figures" (*fukuro jinbutsu*), *Seven Sages of the Bamboo Grove* (15), and the overwhelmingly enormous *Dragons and Clouds* (16), that one can begin to grasp how Yusho's style became established.

Among the unforgettable masterpieces of

15. Seven Sages of the Bamboo Grove

14
The Four Accomplishments

Kaiho Yusho; 10 panels; paper; 186 × 84cm; 16c. ◆

Cultured men pursuing the four arts (calligraphy, music, painting, and the chess-like game of *go*) arts, as depicted by the sages in *The Four Accomplishments,* was an extremely popular theme in Japan. Although this originally decorated an expansive room of the Abbot's Quarters (Hojo), the paintings have since been converted into ten hanging scrolls.

15
Seven Sages of the Bamboo Grove

Kaiho Yusho; paper; vertical dimension 187 × 159.5cm; 16c. ◆

Decorating the Abbot's Quarters (Hojo), *Seven Sages of the Bamboo Grove* has been converted into sixteen hanging scrolls. Seven sages are avoiding worldly affairs and engaging in noble discussion in a bamboo grove, a popular motif of Chinese paintings. The forms of the seven sages are drawn quickly in outline with long brush strokes. Because their clothes are full and billowing in the wind like a bag, these have come to be called "bag figures" (*fukuro jinbutsu*).

Japanese art at Kennin-ji is Tawaraya Sotatsu's (?–?) *Wind God and Thunder God* (17). The gods are painted facing each other, each on its own pair of folding screens. Although there is no signature or seal, there is no doubt who created this magnificent work with its expansive golden background. Depicting only the two gods in a painting had not been done before, and the whimsical, highly ornamental portrayal is very creative. In comparison with Yusho, who was unexpectedly burdened with the weight of a world at war, Sotatsu, who seems to belong to the wealthy and important merchant class, heralds the arrival of the town artist (*machi-e-shi*) with a sense of freedom, light and easy movement, and vivid freshness.

Ito Jakuchu (1716–1800), proprietor of the vegetable shop Masugen in Nishikikoji, Kyoto, turned his inheritance over to his younger brother and decided to devote his life to painting at the age of forty. From then on, he immersed himself in painting every day and, though without a teacher, used Chinese paintings for reference to devise his own style of drawing and painting.

Kyoto during the Edo period was characteristically willing to accept new modes of expression, and Jakuchu's individualistic style was soon accepted as well. He received many orders for work and became a popular painter. Both his painted room partitions at Kinkaku-ji, and Shokoku-ji's *Pictures of the Colorful Realm of Living Beings* are representative masterpieces of one of most favored painters of Zen temples during the Edo period. Jakuchu's pure approach to painting remains fundamentally unchanged, even in deeply pigmented works of concentrated color and uniquely humorous ink portrayals that are not bound by predetermined styles. Such an innocent spirit of painting is the same as the Zen mind, and surely can lead to exchange with Zen priests.

The masterpieces of Soga Shohaku (1730–81), another highly praised, unconventional painter whose works are often compared with Jakuchu's, deserve a special mention. *Landscape Picture* (*Sansui-zu*; 20), a work in the possession of the Kyusho-in sub-temple, is a splendid example of his individual style and sharpness of depiction, and is characteristic of his surrealistic paintings.

Artwork numbered 12, 13, 15~18 entrusted to the Kyoto National Museum.

The Beauty of Great Treasure • 15

16. Dragons and Clouds (detail)

16
Dragons and Clouds
Kaiho Yusho; paper; 198 × 187cm; 16c. ◆

Enormous painting of clouds and dragons in the second reception room of the Abbot's Quarters (Hojo). These paintings of two dragons that are more than two meters tall and span eight sliding screens have been remade into a hanging scroll. Four panels each on the north and west sides, the paintings are not only enormous, but have a three-dimensional aspect, seeming to come towards the viewer.

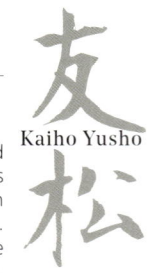

Kaiho Yusho

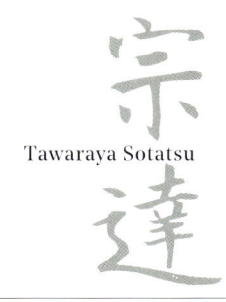

Tawaraya Sotatsu

17

Wind God and Thunder God

Tawaraya Sotatsu; pair of folding screens; paper;
154.5 × 169.8cm (each); 18c. ◆

Sotatsu made effective use of the surrealistic radiance of the
golden background, boldly capturing the movement of the two
deities. The vaguely humorous faces and figures convey a
friendly and light feeling that is not at all intimidating, and there
is a sense of lighthearted buoyancy. Sotatsu's specialty "dripping
in" wet-on-wet paint technique (*tarashikomi*) is put to especially
good use here in the co-mingling of ink and silver in the clouds.

18. Jittoku and Chickens

20

Landscape Picture (Sansui-zu)

Soga Shohaku; silk; 101.6 × 37.6cm (each); 18c.; (Kyusho-in collection)

Mountains towering in the distance, bizarre shapes of rocks, and a sense of peculiar exaggeration give this work a completely surrealistic feel. Shohaku's peculiar technique and form create a unique world within this landscape masterpiece.

19. Plum Tree and Rooster in Snow

若
冲

Ito Jakuchu

18

Jittoku and Chickens

Ito Jakuchu; paper; 101.8 × 28.9cm; 18c.; (Zenkyo-an collection)

There are numerous ink scrolls by Jakuchu, all of which have a humorous aspect and characteristically unique use of ink. The left and right scrolls are chickens, and the center depicts Jittoku, an eccentric Chinese Zen monk who was well-known from numerous paintings. Presenting one's back to the viewer is an interesting technique typical of Jakuchu.

19

Plum Tree and Rooster in Snow

Ito Jakuchu; silk; 113.5 × 56.5cm; 18c.; (Ryosoku-in collection)

Characteristic of the work of self-taught painter Ito Jakuchu are depictions of limitless details and rich colors. In this snowy scene, a rooster pecks the surface of the snow underneath a bush warbler, who rests on white plum blossoms and camellias in full bloom. Such motifs are typical of Jakuchu, who often painted chickens in such lifelike detail, suggesting he kept chickens himself.

20. Landscape Picture (Sansui-zu)

Yotsu-gashira Tea Ceremony to Commemorate Yosai Zenji's Birthday

The Meaning of Yotsu-gashira

The Yotsu-gashira Tea Ceremony has been held at Kennin-ji every year since 1954. It is always held on April 20th in commemoration of the birthday of the temple's founder Yosai, who introduced both Zen and tea to Japan.

The custom of drinking tea became popular in Zen monasteries in China during the Tang dynasty (618–907), and Yosai brought this custom to Japan as the Zen tea ceremony. The ceremony that later became known as Yotsu-gashira was once part of a larger abbot's festival (*hojosai*) that included a meal, however, the event now consists only of tea.

The word *yotsu-gashira* means "four heads," as in this ceremony there are four principal guests instead of the usual one. There are eight guests who accompany each principal guest for a total of thirty-six in each seating. This seating arrangement is strongly reminiscent of the Chinese style. It is possible to see what the Chinese tea ceremony must have been like at the time it was introduced to Japan from the decorations and procedures of the Yotsu-gashira today.

During the Tea Ceremony

The tea ceremony begins, as it has since ancient times, with an incense keeper who offers incense in front of a ceremonial monk's portrait of Yosai, Kennin-ji's founding monk.

Hands pressed together in prayer, the guests take their seats. Next, four monks serving as attendants distribute tea bowls on stands to each guest, along with a box of sweets (22). Each attendant holds a spouted water jug in his left hand and a bamboo whisk (25) in his right, and

21. Tea ceremony decor

prepares tea for each guest, starting with the principal four. A monk kneels on one knee while whisking tea for principal guests and stands, bending slightly at the waist, while whisking for the remaining guests. When the whisking is complete, all guests drink their tea in unison.

When the guests have finished their tea, the four attendant monks collect the tea bowls and sweets containers, and the event concludes with a prayer offered by a monk. The tea ceremony takes about twenty minutes but is conducted, in a very Zen-like manner, in silence from beginning to end with an atmosphere of tension pervading the space.

Yotsu-gashira ceremonies that are open to the public are held at various temples (such as Kencho-ji) in Kamakura. At Kennin-ji, over twenty seatings are held throughout the day, with thirty-six seats available during each; reservations can be made by calling the temple from March first. Aside from this main tea ceremony, other tea events, such as the Fuku-seki (secondary tea ceremony with matcha green tea), Sencha-seki (steeped green tea) and Tenshin-seki (tea with a light meal), are held in the Urasenke and Omotesenke styles at the Reito-in and Kyusho-in sub-temples.

Visiting on this day affords a rare opportunity to see treasures of the sub-temples that are not usually on public display.

21
Tea Ceremony Decor

In the focal point of the room, the ceremonial monk's portrait of Yosai hangs as the central panel of a trio of paintings. On the table in front of the paintings are a candle stand, incense burner, and flower vase, alongside an offering of tea to Yosai.

23. Skillfully Whisking Tea While Standing

22
Techniques of the Attendant Monks

Each of the four attendant monks distributes sweets and tea bowls containing powdered matcha tea to one of the main guests and the accompanying eight guests. They kneel on one knee to place the tea bowl and sweets in front of the main guests and, from a standing position, present the remaining guests with bowls and sweets on a communal tray.

23
Skillfully Whisking Tea While Standing

The attendant monk stands in front of the accompanying guests and pours hot water with his left hand while whisking with his right. Guests raise their tea bowls up to the monks for whisking by holding the stands that support them.

24
Sweets and Tea Bowls with Matcha Tea

Tea bowls already contain matcha powder when they are distributed. The sweets served here are pressed confections in decorative shapes (*monka*) and savory jelly (*konnyaku*).

25
Spouted Water Jug and Bamboo Whisk

The jug is carried with the spout inserted into the whisk.

25. Spouted Water Jug and Bamboo Whisk

22. Techniques of the Attendant Monks

24. Sweets and Tea Bowls with Matcha Tea

Information about Kennin-ji

	Annual Ceremonies and Festivals	
Jan.	1	Early Morning Consecration Service (Dharma Hall)
	2	Sutra Chanting Service (Dharma Hall)
	3	Closing of New Year's Services (Dharma Hall)
Feb.	1	End of Winter Retreat (Training Monastery)
	17	Ceremonies to Commemorate Hyakujo Ekai's Death (Dharma Hall)
March	15	Service to Commemorate Buddha's Death (Dharma Hall)
Apr.	8	Ceremony to Commemorate Buddha's Birthday (Dharma Hall)
	20	Founding Priest's Birthday Celebration and Tea Ceremony (Abbot's Quarters)
May	1	Beginning of Summer Retreat (Training Monastery)
June	5	Founder's Memorial Day and Tea Offering Ceremony (Dharma Hall, Founder's Hall)
July	15	Service for the Benefit of Suffering Spirits (Dharma Hall)
	30	Fusatsue Service for Reflection and Repentance (Abbot's Quarters)
Aug.	1	End of Summer Retreat (Training Monastery)
	18	Memorial Service for second Kamakura Shogun Minamoto no Yoriie (Founder's Hall)
	24	Ceremonies to Commemorate Rankei Doryu's death (Dharma Hall)
Nov.	1	Ceremonies to Commemorate Ankokuji Ekei's death (at the grave of Ankokuji Ekei, Dharma Hall)
		Beginning of Winter Retreat (Training Monastery)
	5	Ceremony Held in Honor of Bodhidharma (Dharma Hall)
	13	Commemoration of the Miraculous Conception of Yosai (Radaimin-jin shrine)
	15	Memorial Ceremonies for Previous Priests (Abbot's Quarters)
		Shido Memorial Service for Parishioners (Abbot's Quarters)
Dec.	1–8	Rohatsu Ozesshin Intensive Winter Meditation (Training Monastery)
	8	Commemoration of Buddha's Enlightenment (Dharma Hall)
	Winter Solstice	Prayers for the Long Life of the Emperor (Dharma Hall)
	31	New Year's Eve (Bell Tower)

Zendo Open to the Public for seated meditation (zazen) sessions and sermons

- **Senko-kai**
  The second Sunday of the month, except for August.
  Early morning seated meditation (zazen) is held in July.
  Time: From 8:00 am to 10:00 am
  Application: Please come to the reception desk of the Main Temple (Honbo)
  about ten minutes before the start of the event
  (prior reservations required for groups).
  Cost: free; only proper intention is required
  Location: the Abbot's Quarters (Hojo) at Kennin-ji
- **Early Morning Seated Meditation (Zazen)**
  Fridays, Saturdays and Sundays during the first ten days of July
  Time: From 6:30 am to 8:00 am
  Application: Please come to the reception desk of the Main Temple (Honbo)
  about ten minutes before the start of the event
  (prior reservations required for groups).
  Free of charge.

Information: info@kenninji.jp

Founder's Memorial Day and
Tea Offering Ceremony

建仁寺インフォメーション

■行事の日程などは変更されることもあるので、あらかじめご確認ください。

おもな年中行事

1月	1日	改旦祝聖（法堂）
	2日	観音懺法（法堂）
	3日	修正満散（法堂）
2月	1日	雪安居解制（僧堂）
	17日	百丈忌（法堂）
3月	15日	涅槃会（法堂）
4月	8日	仏降誕会（法堂）
	20日	開山降誕会　四頭茶会（方丈）
5月	1日	雨安居入制（僧堂）
6月	5日	開山忌　献茶式（法堂　開山堂）
7月	15日	山門施餓鬼（法堂）
	30日	布薩会（方丈）
8月	1日	雨安居解制（僧堂）
	18日	頼家忌（開山堂）
	24日	大覚忌（法堂）
11月	1日	瑶甫忌（安国寺恵瓊首塚　法堂）　雪安居入制（僧堂）
	5日	達磨忌（法堂）
	13日	楽神廟神事（楽大明神）
	15日	先住忌（方丈）　祠堂法要（方丈）
12月	1日〜8日	臘八大接心（僧堂）
	8日	成道会（法堂）
	冬至	冬至祝聖（法堂）
	31日	除夜（鐘楼）

大衆禅堂の開設（坐禅会と法話）

● 千光会　8月を除く毎月第2日曜日（7月は暁天坐禅会を開設）
　時間／午前8時〜10時
　申込み／約10分前まで直接本坊拝観受付へ（団体は要事前連絡）
　費用／個人は無料、団体は志納　場所／建仁寺方丈

● 暁天坐禅会　7月初旬の金、土、日
　時間／午前6時30分〜8時
　申込み／約10分前まで直接本坊拝観受付へ（団体は要事前連絡）
　費用／無料

問い合わせ／建仁寺　e-mail／info@kenninji.jp

よばれる僧が開山栄西の頂相に拝礼するのを合図に始められる。客が合掌して着座すると、よばれる4人の僧によって茶盞と菓子器が配られ（22）、点前（茶を点てる行為）が始まる。供給は左手に浄瓶、右手に茶筅（茶を点てる道具）を持ち、

正客から順番に点てていく。正客には胡跪（片膝をつく座り方）して点前するが、相伴客には立ったまま腰を曲げて行なう（23）。点前が終わったら、皆で一斉に飲む。

飲み終わると、供給が客の菓子器と茶盞を次々と運び出し、僧の拝礼

を最後に式は終了する。およそ20分程度の茶会であるが、禅宗寺院らしく終始無言のうちに行なわれ、方丈には凛とした緊張感が張り詰める。

現在、一般の人が参加できる四頭茶会は、建仁寺のほか鎌倉の建長寺などがある。建仁寺では、3月1日

よばれる僧が開山栄西の頂相に拝礼するのを合図に始められる。供給とよばれる4人の僧によって茶盞と菓子器が配られ

から電話で申し込みを受け付けている。また、塔頭の霊洞院や久昌院などに三千家の副席、煎茶席、点心席が立てられる。

塔頭ではふだん拝観できない寺宝が公開されるので、この日、建仁寺をぜひ訪ねてみたい。

栄西禅師の誕生を祝う四頭茶会

った。江戸時代の京都ならではともいえるが、新しい表現に向き合おうとする寛容さは、まもなく若冲の個性的な表現を受け入れ、若冲は多くの制作依頼が寄せられる人気絵師となったと思われる。鹿苑寺（金閣寺）大書院の障壁画や相国寺（京都市）に寄進された「動植綵絵」が

代表的な大作として知られ、若冲は江戸時代の禅宗寺院に好まれた絵師のひとりであったともいえるだろう。画に対する純粋な姿勢は、執拗なまでに集中力をみせる着色画においても、また、既成の表現にとらわれない、特異でユーモラスな描写の水墨画においても、基本的に変わること

はない。その邪気のない画の精神が禅の心にも通じ、禅僧との交流を導いたものであろうか。また、若冲と並び賞されることの多い奇想の画家、曾我蕭白（１７３０〜８１）の名品の存在についても特筆される。塔頭の久昌院に所蔵される「山水図」（20）は、個性的な

形と描写がとりわけ研ぎ澄まされてみごとであり、独特の超現実的な画世界が確立されている。

---

p.22 「四頭」の意味

建仁寺では、禅と茶を日本に紹介した栄西禅師の遺徳を称え、１９５４年から毎年4月20日の開山降誕会（ごうたんえ）に、四頭茶会（よつがしらちゃかい）を催している。

喫茶の風習は、中国の禅院においては唐代から盛んになったといわれる。栄西はこの風習を、禅院の茶礼❸として日本へ請来した。もとは方丈斎（ほうじょうさい）という食事儀礼の一部であったが、のちに食事の部分が省かれ、茶の作法だけが独立して四頭茶会とよばれるようになった。

「四頭」とは「四主頭（ししゅちょう）」のことで、主位・賓位・主対位・賓対位とよばれ、座位が決められた4人の正客（主賓）をさす。正客はそれぞれ8人の相伴客を伴い、1席で36人が接待を受ける。茶会における4つの座位は、中国的な色合いが強いとされる。飾り付けや作法などに、日本に請来された当時の、中国の茶礼の形態をうかがうことができるという。

p.22 茶会の作法

茶会は古規（禅宗の日常規則）にしたがって、侍香（じこう）と

21. 茶会の室中飾り

22. 供給の作法

23. 立ったまま手際よく茶を点てる

24. 茶菓と抹茶が入った茶盞

25. 浄瓶と茶筅

21. 茶会の室中飾り
会席の正面中央に、栄西の頂相を本尊とする三幅対を掲げる。前卓（まえじょく）の上には燭台や香炉、花瓶と、開山への茶湯が供えられる。

22. 供給の作法
4人の供給がそれぞれ正客ひとりと相伴客8人に菓子と抹茶の入った茶盞を配る。正客には胡跪（こき）して茶碗と菓子器を置き、相伴客へはまとめて運び、立ったままで配る。

23. 立ったまま手際よく茶を点てる
供給は相伴客の前に立って身をかがめ、左手に持った浄瓶から湯を注ぎ、右手の茶筅で茶を点てていく。客は天目台ごと茶碗を捧げるのが作法。

24. 茶菓と抹茶が入った茶盞
客に配られた茶碗には、あらかじめ抹茶が入っている。お菓子は御紋菓とこんにゃく。

25. 浄瓶と茶筅
浄瓶は注ぎ口に茶筅をはめたまま運ばれる。

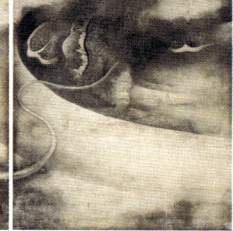

16. 雲龍図（部分）

15. 竹林七賢図（部分）　　　　14. 琴棋書画図（部分）

17. 風神雷神図

19. 雪梅雄鶏図　　　　18. 拾得および鶏図

14. 琴棋書画図

海北友松筆　10幅のうち
紙本　縦186.0×横84.0㎝
桃山時代　◆

賢人たちの4つのたしなみを画題とした「琴棋書画図」は、漢画の画題として日本でも非常に好まれた。方丈の24畳の広さのある上間（じょうかん）一の間を飾った作品で、現在は10幅の掛軸になっている。

15. 竹林七賢図

海北友松筆　16幅のうち
紙本　縦187.0×横159.5㎝
桃山時代　◆

方丈のもっとも広い44畳の室中（しっちゅう）の間を飾っていたのが「竹林七賢図」で、現在は16幅の掛軸になっている。俗事を避けて竹林に遊び、清談をして過ごしたという7賢人を描く漢画の好画題。七賢人の姿は、略筆で一気に長く筆が引かれ、ふっくらとした衣の形をとっており、「袋人物」とも称されている。

16. 雲龍図

海北友松筆　8幅のうち
紙本　各縦198.0×横187.0㎝
桃山時代　◆

方丈の下間（げかん）二の間に描かれた巨大な雲龍図。現在は掛軸に改装されているが、縦2mほどの襖8面にわたって、2匹の龍があらわされていた。4面ずつ北側と西側にはめ込まれていたもので、巨大であるばかりでなく、立体的に観る者に迫ってきたことであろう。

17. 風神雷神図

俵屋宗達筆　屏風　二曲一双
紙本　各縦154.5×横169.8㎝
江戸時代

宗達は、金地の超現実的な輝きを十分に生かして、動きのある2神像を大胆に描き出

した。どことなくユーモラスな面貌や姿には親しみやすい軽味があって、けっして人を威圧することなく飄々（ひょうひょう）とした感覚である。宗達が得意とした描法で、絵の具の自然なにじみを利用した「たらしこみ」は、ここで墨と銀を交えた雲の表現に用いられて効果的である。

18. 拾得（じっとく）および鶏図

伊藤若冲筆　紙本
各縦101.8×横28.9㎝
江戸時代　禅居庵

若冲はこのような水墨画の掛軸を多く残しているが、どれもユーモラスな形と独特の墨の用法が特徴である。左右は鶏、中央は「寒山拾得図」の画題で有名な、奇行の多いふたりの中国の禅僧のうちの拾得。後ろ向きに描かれているところが若冲らしくおもしろい。

19. 雪梅雄鶏図（せつばいゆうけいず）

伊藤若冲筆　絹本
縦113.5×横56.5㎝
江戸時代　両足院

独自の画法を貫いた絵師伊藤若冲の着色画は、限りなく詳細な描写と彩色が特徴である。鶏を飼ってその姿を観察し、作品にすることも多かった若冲らしい主題で、白梅にとまる鶯（うぐいす）と椿（つばき）の咲く雪景に、雪面をついばむ1羽の雄鶏を描いている。

20. 山水図

曾我蕭白筆　絹本
各縦101.6×横37.6㎝
江戸時代　久昌院

遠くに屹立（きつりつ）する山や奇怪な岩の形など、誇張された独特の造形感覚はまるでシュールレアリスム絵画のよう。個性的な描法と形で絵画世界を構築する蕭白の山水画の傑作。

20. 山水図

12. 十六羅漢図 注荼半託迦尊者（左）
13. 十六羅漢図 因掲陀尊者（右）

12. 十六羅漢図 注荼半託迦尊者
13. 十六羅漢図 因掲陀尊者

良全筆　絹本　各縦143.2×横59.6㎝
南北朝時代　◆
良全は、東福寺の仏画制作を専門とした絵師で、同寺の有名な画僧明兆（みんちょう 1351〜1431）に先行する立場にあった。16幅のそれぞれにひとりの羅漢を描いて十六羅漢とした作品で、図柄は典型的であるものの、重厚な迫力のある描写が魅力的な傑作である。右が第13尊者の因掲陀（いんがだ）、左が第16尊者の注荼半託迦（ちゅうだはんたか）。

れる渡来僧に、建仁寺第11世住持持蘭渓道隆と一山一寧（1247〜131 7）がいる。蘭渓は34歳で来日、鎌倉幕府執権北条時頼（1227〜6 3）の帰依を受けて、鎌倉の建長寺の開山に迎えられている。蘭渓所用とされる袈裟は、弟子たちを厳しい規律によって指導し、質朴な禅風で知られた蘭渓の精神を今に伝える。

一山一寧もまた鎌倉の寺と縁深く、北条貞時（1271〜1311）の帰依を受けて建長寺に入った。建仁寺に伝えられる墨蹟「雪夜作」は、13 15年に一山が京都南禅寺第三世住持に迎えられていたころにつくった1編の詩である。禅宗二祖（二番目の祖）慧可（えか）（487〜593）が腰まで埋

まるほどの雪の中で、禅宗の開祖達磨大師（?〜?）に入門を請うたという逸話などが詠み込まれている。

建仁寺の「十六羅漢図」（12、13）は、日本の代表的な羅漢図（釈迦が涅槃に入るとき教えを託された聖者を描いた図）の名品で、中国の作品を手本とした標準的な図様を示している。作者は東福寺（京都市）の絵仏師良全（?〜?）。東福寺に重用され、十六羅漢が勧進されていたとの記録もある。図中に「東福寺常住」と金泥で書かれていることからも、かつて東福寺で制作され、所蔵されていたことがわかる。

p.14

4人の奇才絵師
友松、宗達、若冲、蕭白

近江（滋賀県）の戦国大名浅井氏の重臣の家に生まれた海北友松（15 33〜1615）が、絵師を志したのは戦乱の世と無関係ではなかったものと推察されている。1573年に浅井家が滅亡したときに、海北家で唯一残ったのが当時出家していた友松であった。その後、武将にも僧にもならず、絵師の道を選んだのは友松にとって生きるための選択であった。

狩野派（日本の画壇に君臨した最大画派）正系の画法を学んだらしい友松は、やがて有名な中国人絵師の様式を取り入れながら、みずからの画風を確立し、この時代の重要な絵師のひとりとなった。

1599年に建仁寺の方丈が再建されたとき、友松はすでに67歳。当時としては高齢の絵師であった。しかし、どちらかといえば晩成型の友松が、狩野派を脱してみずからの境地を大成しようとするその重要な展開期にあって、全50面に及ぶ方丈の襖絵制作の意義は大きい。そのなかには、「琴棋書画図」（14）のような狩野派の画法に近い作品もあるが、「袋人物」とも称される略

階級に属したといわれる宗達は、その表現においても自由闊達であり、軽やかに、また鮮烈に町絵師の時代の到来を告げているのである。

京都錦小路の青物問屋「枡源（ますげん）」の主人であった伊藤若冲（1716〜1800）が、家督を弟に譲り、絵師の道に専念したのは1755年、40歳のときであった。それからは絵画制作に没頭する日々で、特定の師をもたず、中国画などを参照しながら、独自の形と描法を編み出してい

筆の大らかな描写が特徴となっている「竹林七賢図」（15）や、まずその大きさで圧倒する「雲龍図」（16）など、友松様式が立ちあらわれようとしていることが見て取れる。

建仁寺は、日本美術の名品中の名品、俵屋宗達（?〜?）の「風神雷神図」（17）が所蔵されることで知られる。二曲一双の金地屏風で、風神と雷神が対峙するように描かれる。作品には署名も印章もないが、この開放感ある金地の華麗な作品の筆者を疑う者はいないだろう。風神雷神だけを取り出して描いた絵画はこれ以前にはなく、軽味のある装飾性の高い描写も独創的だ。はからずも戦乱の世の重みを背負ってしまった友松とは対照的に、富裕な町衆階級に属したといわれる宗達は、その……

7. 法堂 江戸時代

（両手の手指であらわした形）は、坐禅して瞑想する姿をあらわす禅定印を結ぶ。脇侍は、釈迦十大弟子のうち、「頭陀（煩悩を除去する）第一」といわれた摩訶迦葉と、「多聞（仏法を多く聞き知っている）第一」といわれた阿難の組み合わせで、禅宗寺院に多く見られる。

建仁寺の仏殿は、1552年の兵火で類焼し、その後、再建されなかったため、現在まで法堂が仏殿として兼用されている。正面に本尊釈迦如来坐像と脇侍の摩訶迦葉・阿難立像を安置。脇壇の祖師堂には栄西像などが祀られている。

p.8 法堂（7）

棟札により、1765年の建立とされる。桁行5間（幅約9m）、梁間4間（高さ約7・2m）で、花頭窓（火灯形の窓）、桟唐戸などに禅宗様建築の特徴が見られる。釈迦の法を以心伝心で受け継いだ摩訶迦葉の「拈華微笑」❹の故事にちなみに、「拈華堂」ともよばれ、大きく

p.10 開山堂（9）

開山栄西禅師❺の塔所（墓所）として、1884年に竣工。平面が凸字形で、前方から礼堂・相の間・祠堂で構成される。礼堂は正面7間（約12・6m）、側面3間（約5・5m）、入母屋造り、本瓦葺き。相の間には開山の入定塔（墓所）があり、最奥の祠堂に開山である栄西の木像を安置する。

開山堂（9）の正面には「宝陀閣」とよばれる楼門が聳える。開山堂の建造に合わせて、1885年に妙光寺（京都市）から移築された。江戸時代中期の建立とされ、階上に上がるための山廊（山門の両脇にある平屋の建物）を備える。前庭には、栄西が宋から持ち帰って植えたと伝えられる3本の菩提樹が残る。寺のもっとも重要な霊域として、つねに厳粛な気が漂う。通常、内部は非公開のため、柵外から山門の宝陀閣を望むだけとなる。

10. 開山堂内部

9. 開山堂 明治時代

10. 開山堂内部
床には甎（せん 煉瓦）が敷き詰められ、中央にたこ足の香炉が置かれる。相の間の石壇上に、木柵で結界を巡らした開山の入定塔があり、灯火が昼夜ともされている。開山像は背後の階段上に安置され、階段下の脇壇に開基源頼家の坐像（3）が祀られている。

11. 栄西禅師像
木造 像高130.8cm 江戸時代
裳裾（もすそ）裏の朱漆の銘により、1664年に慶派（平安時代末から江戸時代に活躍した仏師の一派）の大仏師康乗（こうじょう）が造像したと知られる。法衣に鐶裂裟（わげさ）を付けて曲彔（きょくろく 法会の際に僧が用いる椅子）に座り、右手には払子（ほっす 法具のひとつ）を執る通例の頂相形式を示す。

11. 栄西禅師像

鎌倉時代初期に禅宗が伝えられると、禅は武家をはじめとする上層階級の精神のよりどころとなり、同時にその美意識は、書や水墨画、建築などに深く影響した。初期の日本の禅宗における重要な存在として知ら

解説●田辺昌子（千葉市美術館副館長）

4. 明庵栄西像

4. 明庵(みんなん)栄西像
絹本 縦93.0×横38.5cm
室町時代 両足院
開山栄西の頂相(ちんそう 禅僧の肖像画)として現存最古のものとされる。相国寺の住持絶海中津(ぜっかいちゅうしん 1334～1405)が、円覚寺(鎌倉市)開山無学祖元(むがくそげん 1226～86)の作を引用して賛を記している。

府の衰退とともに経済力を失い、荒廃する伽藍の維持は困難を極める。その後も幾度となく危機に直面するが、栄西の法灯を守りぬいた。宗門一致団結し、栄西の法灯を守りぬいた。

栄西はまた、中国の禅院で盛んだった茶礼(されい)❸を伝えたことでも名高い。茶の種を持ち帰り、栽培や喫茶の法を人々に伝授し、茶祖として尊崇されている。

の門弟は2000人、孫弟子は1万人にも及んだという。1259年、蘭渓道隆(らんけいどうりゅう)(1213～78)が第11世住持(住職)になったとき、建仁寺は兼宗禅から純粋禅の道場に改められた。室町時代には、3代将軍足利義満(あしかがよしみつ)(1358～1408)によって京都五山第3位に列せられ、最盛期を迎える。五山文学が花開き、多くの高僧が輩出した。

しかし室町時代のなかばには、幕

p.6
兼宗禅から純粋禅の道場へ

1215年、74歳で示寂した栄西

で、同じく年号を寺号とする延暦寺と同様の官寺であったとされる。当初は比叡山をはばかり、禅宗、真言宗、天台宗の3宗兼学を旨とした。栄西は質素な暮らしをしながらも、貧しい人から救いを求められると、本堂の薬師如来の光背(こうはい)❷を折り取って与え、弟子に呆れられたという。

p.8

本尊讃歌

8. 釈迦如来坐像

8. 釈迦如来坐像
木造 像高90.8cm 室町時代
結跏趺坐し、腹前で両手を重ね合わせる禅定印を結ぶ。禅定に入って瞑想する姿は安定感があり、深いまなざしに心が静まる。16世紀後半に越前(福井県)の弘祥寺(こうしょうじ)から移されたものと伝えられる。

平安末期、当時の仏教界の退廃を嘆いた栄西は、中国から禅を持ち帰り、日本仏教界に清風を吹き込んだ。

禅宗では、仏教の開祖である釈迦への回帰を強く希求し、釈迦を修行完成の模範とする。坐禅を修行の中心とするのも、若き日の釈迦が苦行をやめて禅定(ぜんじょう)(精神を集中して瞑想するだ座り方)に入り、そこで悟りに達し

たことにならい、坐禅によって悟りを開くことを重んじるからである。それゆえ、おもに臨済宗寺院では、修行する姿をあらわす在俗の釈迦像が重んじられ、本尊として安置されることが多い。

法堂(仏の教えを講義する建物)に祀られる本尊は、結跏趺坐(けっかふざ)(両足を組んだ座り方)の釈迦如来坐像(8)。印相

5. 大雄苑(方丈前庭)

5. 大雄苑(だいおうえん)(方丈前庭)
広く白砂が敷き詰められ、背後に配された植栽と巨石との対比が美しい。「大雄苑」の名は、中国中南部の江西省(こうせいしょう)にある百丈山(ひゃくじょうざん)の別名である大雄峰にちなむ。

6. 茶室「東陽坊(とうようぼう)」
方丈の北にある茶室。近くに、割り竹をすきまなく縦に並べ、二つ割りにした竹を横にあてがって編んだ閑雅な風情の「建仁寺垣」がある。

6. 茶室「東陽坊」

祇園の花見小路の石畳を歩んでいくと、建仁寺の渋い土塀があらわれ、自然と境内にいざなわれる。

建仁寺は、京都最古の禅寺として、800年余りの歴史を誇る。正式には、臨済宗建仁寺派大本山東山建仁寺という。観光名所として名高い八坂神社や円山公園にほど近く、周辺には年間を通じて観光客が絶えない。花街である祇園と隣り合わせに建ち、厳しい修行で知られる禅寺との取り合わせが愉快にも思える。

町中にもかかわらず、境内はのびやかに広く、お茶の木や松の緑がすがすがしい。その中心に、禅宗寺院特有の伽藍（建物）が南北に建ち並ぶ。周囲を荘厳な雰囲気の開山堂や塔頭 ❶寺院がものものしく取り囲み、いまもなお、禅の修行道場としての伝統を感じ取ることができる。

中国から禅を請来した栄西

p.2

建仁寺の開山（お寺を開いた僧）栄西〔えいさい〕とも読む〕（4）は、1141年備中（岡山県）吉備津神社（岡山市）の神職の子として生まれた。父のもとで仏教の素養を身につけ、8歳でインドの仏教論書を読んだという。その後天台教学を学び、14歳で京都北部の比叡山にある天台宗総本山延暦寺で教えを受けた。

源平の争乱が続く平安時代（79４～1185）末期、世の中は末法（仏の教えがすたれ、世の中が混乱のきわみになる）の様相を呈していた。本来ならば正しい教えを実践し手本となるべき比叡山は、皇族・貴族の子弟が入寺して生活の貴族化が進むいっぽう、教団内では権力争いが続けられた。こうした比叡山の世俗化は、仏法を求めてやってきた者たちを失望させた。栄西は釈迦への回帰、仏教の原点に戻る必要性を痛感し、真の仏法を求めて中国（宋）に渡ることを決意する。

1168年、28歳で初めて中国に渡った栄西は、臨済禅の盛んである禅のに深い感銘を受けるが、わずか6か月間の滞在で帰国。47歳で再び中国ことになる。

国を訪れた栄西は、臨済宗黄龍派の虚庵懐敞〔きあんえじょう〕を訪ねた。そして虚庵のもと、4年にわたって黄龍派の禅を学び、ついに臨済宗黄龍派の伝法を許された。

帰国した栄西は、肥前〔ひぜん〕（長崎県）平戸〔ど〕に入り、日本で初めて禅規（禅宗の規範による生活）を行なった。

その後、栄西は都で布教を開始するが、比叡山などの旧仏教勢力に阻まれ、朝廷から禅宗停止を命じられる。やむなく九州に4年間とどまったのち、武家の本拠地である鎌倉へと向かった。新しい禅の教えは武士の気風に合い、絶大な帰依を受ける

鎌倉幕府との関係

p.4

栄西は鎌倉幕府2代将軍 源頼家〔いえ〕（1182～1204）（3）に深く信頼されるとともに、1200年には初代将軍の正室北条政子〔ほうじょうまさこ〕（1157～1225）の発願で寿福寺（鎌倉市）の開山に迎えられる。頼家を開基（創立者）に、1202年、ついに京に建仁寺を建立するにいたった。寺号の「建仁」は朝廷から贈られたもの

1. 勅使門

2. 法堂天井画の双龍図

3. 開基源頼家像

木造　像高73.6cm　江戸時代
21歳で鎌倉幕府2代将軍に就いた源頼家の坐像。建仁寺の開基として開山堂に祀られる。像は550年遠忌にあたって1752年に造像され、翌年に開眼供養が営まれたという。

3. 開基源頼家像

1. 勅使門（ちょくしもん）

鎌倉時代　◆
切妻（きりづま）造り、銅板葺きの四脚門。

2. 法堂天井画の双龍図

創建800年を記念して、2002年、日本画家の小泉淳作(1924～2012)画伯が制作。画面は縦11.4m、横15.7m、108畳分という。双龍は阿吽（あうん）像とされ、2匹が協力して仏法を守護する姿をあらわすという。

建仁寺の歴史

時代区分	西暦	おもなできごと
鎌倉 1185〜1333	1202	中国（宋）から帰国した栄西が、鎌倉幕府2代将軍 源 頼家の庇護を受けて創建。当初は、禅宗のほか天台宗・真言宗を兼学する修行場だった。
鎌倉 1185〜1333	1205	伽藍（建物）が竣工し、官寺となる。
鎌倉 1185〜1333	1215	栄西、建仁寺（一説に鎌倉寿福寺）で示寂（他界）。
鎌倉 1185〜1333	1246	蘭渓道隆が来日。
鎌倉 1185〜1333	1258	第10世住持円爾弁円が、諸堂を復興する。
室町 1336〜1573	1342	幕府により京都五山の第4位となる。
室町 1336〜1573	1386	五山改定により京都五山の第3位となる。
室町 1336〜1573	1469	応仁・文明の乱の兵火により焼失。
室町 1336〜1573	1552	戦により伽藍が全焼、塔頭の多くも失われる。
安土桃山 1573〜1603	1586	豊臣秀吉より、寺領820石を寄進される。
江戸 1603〜1868	1614	徳川家康より、寺領820石を寄進される。
明治 1868〜1912	1872	京都五山と大徳寺・妙心寺が団結し7派と称することとなる。以後、建仁寺派を名乗る。初代管長に荊叟東玳が就任。
昭和 1926〜1989	1934	室戸台風により方丈が倒壊するなど、山内が大きな被害を受ける。
昭和 1926〜1989	1964	開山栄西禅師750年遠忌を営む。
平成 1989〜2019	2002	開創800年記念として、法堂天井画「双龍図」の開眼法要を営む。

用語解説

① 塔頭（たっちゅう）

おもな仏教寺院の境内周辺にある子院・末寺のこと。もとは高僧の墓から発展したが、現在のほとんどの塔頭は高名な僧侶の住まいもしくは貴族の菩提寺として始まった。

② 光背（こうはい）

仏像の背後にある飾りで、仏の身体から発する光を象徴的に表現したもの。

③ 茶礼（されい）

禅僧の集団修行生活に欠かせない儀式のひとつ。修行の一環として日に数度行われる。

④ 拈華微笑（ねんげみしょう）

宗の起源を説く故事のひとつ。釈迦が人々に対して無言で蓮華を拈（ひね）って見せたとき、皆はその意味がわからずただ黙っていたが、弟子の摩訶迦葉（まかかしょう）だけは理解して微笑（ほほえ）んだという。言葉にはできない仏教の真理が、迦葉にだけは無言のままに伝授されたことから、禅宗で、以心伝心で法を会得することを示す語として用いられる。

⑤ 禅師（ぜんじ）

禅宗の高僧に対する敬称。とくに朝廷から禅師号を賜った者をさす。

本書の表記について

この本は、京都の禅寺・建仁寺について紹介しています。◆は国宝、◆は重要文化財をあらわしています。用語解説が必要な語句については、注釈番号を付しており、英語での解説は1ページに、日本語での解説は32ページに掲載しました。仏教用語などの専門的な日本語はローマ字読みにし、アルファベットで表記しています。また、本文中の人物名は英語も日本語と同様に姓名の順で表記しました。年齢は数え年で表記しています。